Fun on the Run!

A Scholastic Peek at the New York City Marathon

by

Fiona Bayly

This book is a non-fiction account of the author's experiences and observations. Any resemblance to actual persons, living or dead, is coincidental.

ISBN: 1-4107-2399-2 (e-book)
ISBN: 1-4107-2400-X (Paperback)
ISBN: 1-4107-2401-8 (Hardcover)

This book is printed on acid free paper.

® The New York City Marathon is a registered trademark. The New York City Marathon is organized and produced by the New York Road Runners, a not-for-profit international establishment and community educator. Website: www.nyrrc.org.

1stBooks - rev. 6/9/03

DEDICATION

This creation is dedicated to the memory of my former boss and neighborhood celebrity, Fred Lebow, and to the many courageous, creative immigrants who, like Fred, made their way to the United States of America and made beneficial contributions to the nation's excellent goals of individual freedom and international peace.

It is impossible for me to name every additional person whose character or examples inspired me to write this book. However, among those I feel I must name here are my loving family; my loyal friends – many of whom now have children of their own; my former colleagues at the New York Road Runners Club and at the Metropolitan Museum of Art; my inspiring colleagues at the Wildlife Conservation Society/Bronx Zoo; my amazing New York City neighbors (and my good landlord!), and my many, hilarious fellow runners. In addition, I must pay my deepest respects to those physicians, humanists, scientists and artists who continue to improve the health of all kinds of animals and organisms, humans included; and to all the volunteers throughout the world – not just at road races – who give, selflessly, their time, effort and assistance to friends and strangers alike.

To all who share a passion for this vital, ageless sport
That always has embraced the young, the old, the tall, the short,
The greatest of its lessons is to carefully explore
Life's many possibilities – and then explore some more.

The New York City Marathon is famous for its fun!
A couple million people love the day the race is run;
They know it's long – the race is almost twenty-
seven miles
But sports fans cheer from every street and give
the runners smiles.

Runners who have planned the trip from all around
the world,
They come to New York City, and with printed maps
unfurled
Embark upon a journey through five boroughs – on
their feet! -
And finish up in Central Park, Manhattan's garden
sweet.

Marathon Missions

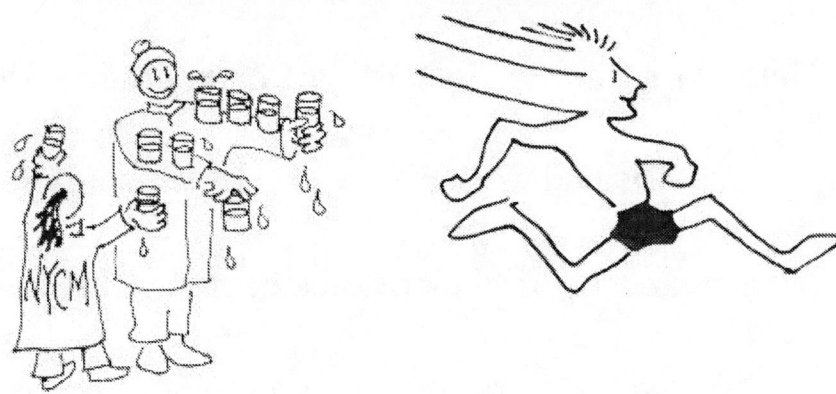

The runners aren't the only ones who love this
wondrous race:
The volunteers and staff and crews have their
important place,
And lots of people who don't run are key in other
ways;
They put their skills to work in many marathon
métiers.

That's French for "occupations" or in other words,
"careers,"
The jobs and work we do; and be we paid or
volunteer
We make a map of choices, like cartographers who
chart
A city's roads and waterways – and where our race
will start.

1. Staten Island
2. Brooklyn
3. Queens
4. Manhattan
5. Bronx

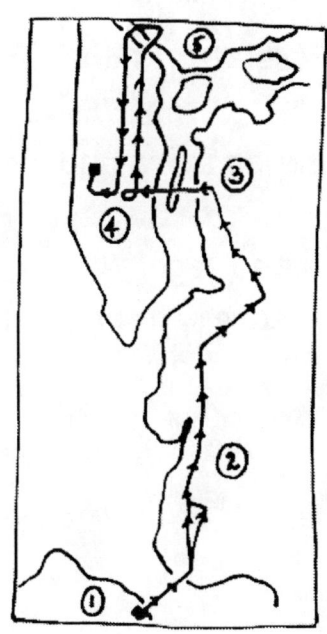

Fiona Bayly

Marathons are rather like those Broadway shows,
you know.
The race director organizes just where things will
go,
Is helped by clever managers to stage this sell-out
"play,"
And bravely makes a thousand new decisions every
day.

And often what's decided is by teamwork, this is
true,
A team of good assistants and financial wizards,
too,
And engineers and doctors and musicians and the
firms
Which cover all the legal things, like rules and
safety terms.

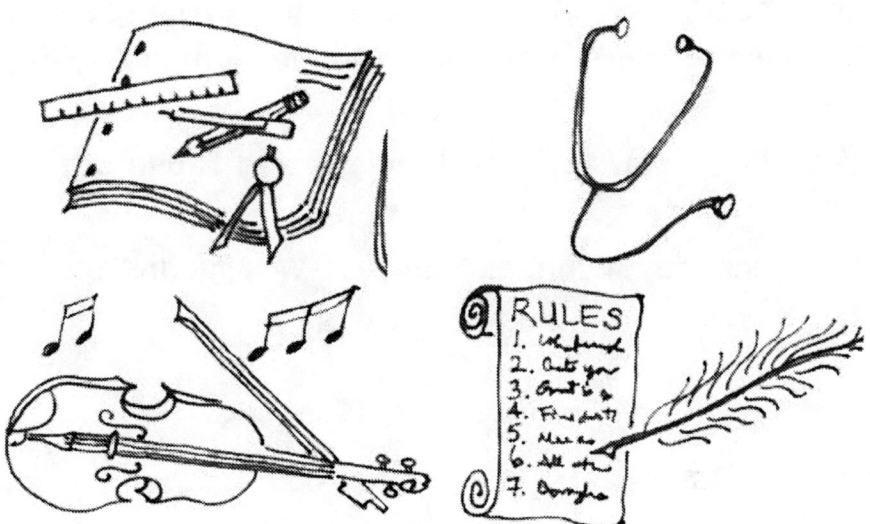

Then come the artists, advertisers, city personnel,
The firefighters and police (police-dogs – ARFFF! –
as well)
And road crews and technicians and those patient
traffic-cops
(On race-day, runners' right-of-way means traffic
has new stops).

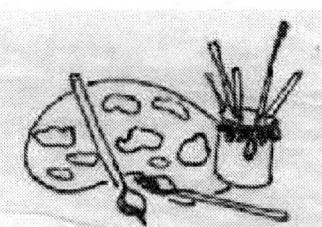

The Mayor of the city and the race director talk
About the race-course usage of the city streets, sidewalks
And parks. They ask commissioners for good advice and tips
On how to keep the pretty gardens free from nasal strips.

(A nasal strip's a tiny band that pulls across the nose
In case it helps a runner breathe. And does it work? Who knows!)

Fiona Bayly

The marathon has clothes designers, scientists and
cooks,
Merchandisers, travel agents, authors of those
books

About the proper training runners always have to
do
To keep from getting injured and to feel as good as
new –
And books on travel, sure, because we run
throughout the world
From snowy lands to sandy isles across the oceans
swirled.

Fiona Bayly

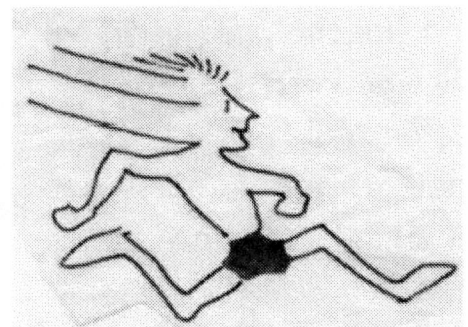

Marathon Mechanics

One often hears the word "mechanics" meaning
workers who
Deal closely with machines or tools or engines old
and new.
In marathons, however, the machines have human
shape
With moving parts, skin, limbs and hearts. No need
for electrical tape.

Mechanics help describe a runner's action as they
move;
Mechanics help a runner get efficient, "in the
groove."
The easier the movement flows, the more one's
energy
Can feed quick speed or power; that's called good
efficiency.

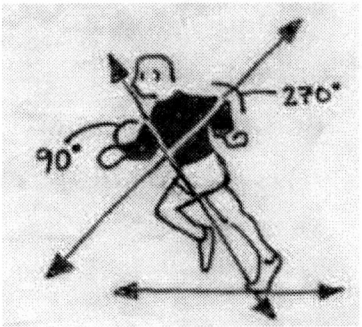

It's good to bend the knees, and landing softly
helps a lot,
Not on the heels but mid-foot. That's how best to
spread the shock.
The arms should not be held down stiff, nor
reaching too far out;
They swing aside the torso quite relaxed. It's all
about

A looseness and a balance so it feels like flying –
though
One must admit it's sometimes difficult and
sometimes slow –
But that's OK, since after all, machines might
sometimes rust
And bodies, like machines, must get good
maintenance. They must.

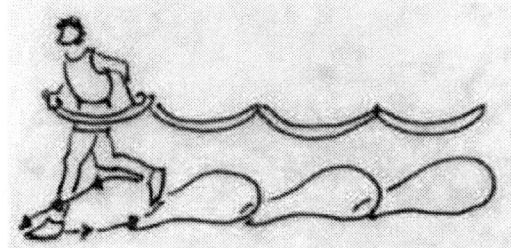

Fiona Bayly

Marathon

Medicine

So, that's where doctors play a part in treating runners sore.
Sports doctors and psychiatrists, podiatrists and more,
To deal with bumps and worries, nerves, and twisted ankle sprains;
The medics, they are trained to help one heal beyond the pain.

Sometimes a cooling ointment makes a scraped
knee feel quite nice
But hot swelling and sore redness will require some
chilling ice.
A little scratch may only need a bandage to protect
(And if one's butt gets stuck in a rut, do *gently*
stand erect!).

The foot is so important, be it large or be it small,
That doctors called podiatrists give it pretty much
their all;
They laud the foot's construction as amazing,
strong and neat,
Designed to spring and cushion – Yes, a foot's a
mechanical feat.

Most runners will not smoke, for they know smoking
harms the lungs,
And smoking hurts their hearts, their bones, their
throats, their tasteful tongues.
Most runners know good sleep will also help their
health be fun,
For rest does heal the muscles from the many miles
they've run.

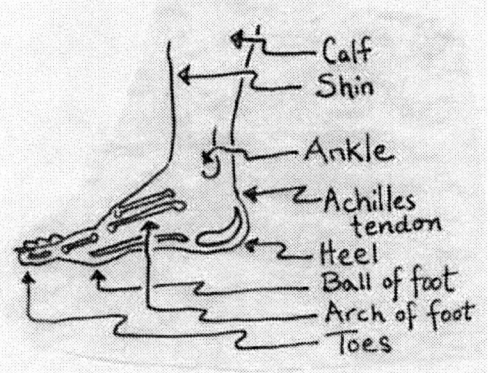

Calf
Shin
Ankle
Achilles
tendon
Heel
Ball of foot
Arch of foot
Toes

Fiona Bayly

Marathon Munchies

Along with rest is eating. Now, nutrition deals with
food.
Nutritionists can study food's support of health
and mood,
These scientists research how proper eating can
help most,
Through breakfast muffins, scrambled eggs, or
slightly burned rye toast,

Or lunch: perhaps a sandwich of tomatoes, tuna and
Green lettuce, packed with vitamins. Or if you
cannot stand
A sandwich, go for yogurt topped with nuts or
sweet, sliced fruit.
Such items and such meals are what nutritionists
recruit.

It's funny when a runner has to eat while in a race;
The trick is staying upright with a food-thing in
one's face!
In fact, unless one practices just where that
munchie goes,
The danger then becomes of getting mustard up
one's nose.

Nutrition is important, and the better foods to
know
Are fruits and eggs and vegetables and breads
from whole wheat dough,
And nuts and soup and yogurt, also tofu (soybean
stuff)
And honey. But do stay away from fake
marshmallow fluff.

Fiona Bayly

Marathon Music

Fiona Bayly

The music in the marathon depends on what's
around:
The drumbeat of the runners' feet while pounding
on the ground
Is echoed in the bands whose bang-up-brilliant
drummers play,
And whose flutes, guitars and trumpets sing to
celebrate the day.

A band at every mile is New York City's
atmosphere!
Musicians form a festival of rhythms, songs and
cheers;
They keep the spirits high and spread enjoyment
through the crowd,
They soothe, inspire, invigorate and make the
runners proud.

Fiona Bayly

Marathon Meteorology

Fiona Bayly

Let's not forget the music of the heavens: it's the
weather!
If rain, it might roll in on thunderous wing and
ruffled feather;
If snow, it floats down cold and white, transported
by the air;
If calm prevails (neither sleet nor hail) one calls
the weather "fair."

Of course, the weather also can be strangely very
warm,
For even in November, when one might expect a
storm
Some days are warm and toasty, almost roasty,
with a sun
That seems to have forgot that summertime has
long been done.

41

Fiona Bayly

Marathon

Money

And while we're on the subject of things falling
from the sky,
Do pennies fall from heaven? Almost never. Here is
why:
Most pennies, like most coins, are manufactured
here on earth,
Then assigned a certain value which, in turn,
determines worth.

Financial specialists are who the race directors
need
To help coordinate the costs of measuring race-
speed.
It can get quite expensive, buying high-
performance clocks
And paying all the staffers, and supplying extra
socks,

Providing health insurance, proper salaries and
such;
Controlling costs and advertising ... Finance counts
so much!
But money, though supportive, never is the
greatest prize;

It's always more important what one does, not what one buys.

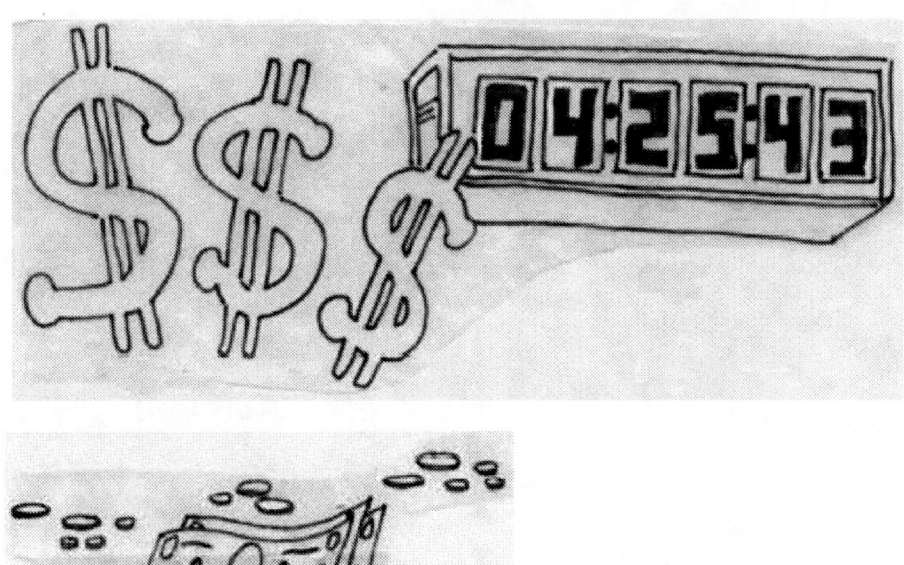

Fiona Bayly

Marathon Mathematics

Mathematics is a special part of many runners'
lives:
To measure distance they must know their ones,
twos, threes, fours, fives.
They must read time correctly if they want to
figure "pace"
(How fast they're really running) in a practice or a
race.

They have to know addition when it's time to count
their feet.
Sometimes a runner has just one; their one foot is
so fleet
They *wear* another, springing fast, as graceful as
can be...
And just imagine if a runner's foot-count equaled...
three!

Fiona Bayly

A runner knows subtraction, too, as on those days
so hot
They must subtract their coat or take away what
else they've got,
To keep a comfy temperature. Thermometers are
fun –
They're all about the measure of degrees, just one
by one.

And clocks have much division, see, as minutes,
seconds, hours
Divide into each other with such perfect
mathematical powers.
In racing, we call "splits" those sections making up
the time
A runner spends in one event, their total "Finish
time."

The marathon has numbers, numbers, numbers and
still more,
And someone has to keep their eye on demographic
lore;
The demographic values, called "statistics,"
illustrate
The marathon's amazing wealth of scientific
freight.

There are thirty thousand runners, and four times
as many pins,
And sixty thousand legs - if we were fish, we'd
count our fins -
Some thirty thousand good bananas, protein bars
and gels

(The gels taste like thick icing and have different, fruity smells).

Fiona Bayly

And think: if every runner has ten fingers and ten
toes
Six hundred thousand digits make the journey. And
who knows
How many freckles make the trip!? We'll never
know for sure
But statisticians love this stuff – they'll always ask
for more:

The runners' nationalities, their occupations, ages,
Their education, married state, perhaps their
working wages.
Such demographics prove what runners all believe
in kind:
The sport is democratic; not a soul is left behind.

Fiona Bayly

MARATHON

MAPPING

The New York City Marathon is special, for it goes
Through each and every hamlet (also known as "The
Five Boroughs").
First: Staten Island, long ago, was founded by the
Dutch
As farming land all tilled by hand, and so much
prized as such

The Duke of York awarded it to winners of a race
Of sailing boats! The island was the prize, and now's
the place
Where marathoners start. The Verrazano-Narrows
Bridge
Provides the road across the water, rising as a
ridge

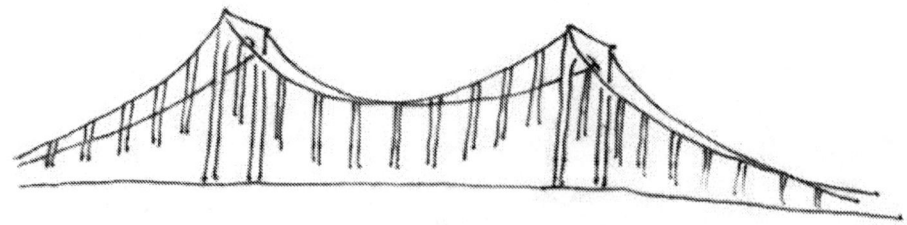

And then descending into Brooklyn, beautiful and
old,
The borough with most people has the longest
stretch, all told,
Of twelve quick miles through Bay Ridge, where
ancestors were the Norse,
Then Sunset Park, where Asians and Hispanics line
the course.

Then soon to Muslim neighborhoods, the Brooklyn
Dodgers' land,
And Bedford-Stuyvesant, where African-
Americans
With glorious, great music love the runners coming
through
Who soon run into Williamsburg, where live Hasidic
Jews;

Then Greenpoint, largely Polish; the Pulaski Bridge
will mark
The halfway-point! Another thirteen miles to
Central Park!
Across the bridge is Queens, so named for
Catherine, you know,
A Spanish queen who married England's Charles the
Second. So,

Fiona Bayly

Across the Queensboro Bridge, the wide East River
underneath,
Comes grand Manhattan, "Isle of Hills." Algonquins
did bequeath
That lovely name to what became, years later,
freedom's door,
America's famed entry-point for people rich and
poor

From many other nations seeking better life and
hope.
The immigrants had dreams, worked hard and
helped each other cope.
Hungarians and Germans, Czechs and Slovaks, Irish,
too,
Italians, French and Africans – A "melting pot," a
stew

Of languages and culture – just imagine all the
trade!
Manhattan's civil courts were where the politicians
played
And uptown Harlem's artists played great ragtime,
gospels, jazz –
Historically the city's lore is steeped in
razzmatazz.

But back to running marathons. My goodness, how
time flies!
The runners reach the bridge at Willis Avenue –
Surprise!
Behold, a bright red carpet, placed down gently on
the grates.
Such royal treatment makes each runner feel like
Grete Waitz!

See, Grete is a famous lass, a champion for all
Who ever dream of marathoning in the midst of
fall;
She won the New York race nine times with
courage and with style,
She also won the people's admiration, every mile.

Now, to continue: Since the race has left
Manhattan's way,
The runners reach "The Bronx," named after Jonas
Bronck, they say,
Who settled by the river back in 1639,
Three centuries before the baseball Yankees built
their shrine.

The stadium is near the route; the runners pass
quite close.
By now, however, maybe they are staring at their
toes...
Until they hear a gospel choir; how Harlem's
children sing!
Their songs fly along and give each runner's heel an
extra wing!

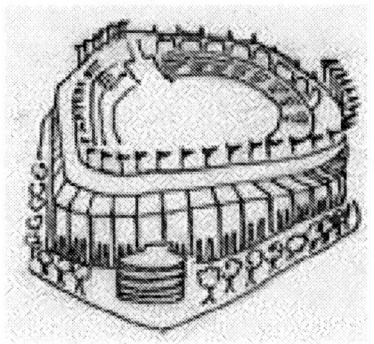

And soon, at mile twenty-two the runners carry
through
Back into cool Manhattan, running down Fifth
Avenue
And entering sweet, verdant, green and golden
Central Park
With crowds a-cheering madly at the twenty-four
mile mark

Where stands "Fred Lebow Way," named for the
founder of this race.
The course unfolds its last few yards; the runners
still give chase
To reach the Finish by the famous Tavern-on-the-
Green,
Exhausted yet triumphant, with the biggest smiles
you've seen.

Fiona Bayly

The runners greet each other, or they celebrate
around,
Or simply walk real slowly – some will even kiss the
ground.
They eat and drink and find their friends, and plan
to have a rest;
They know that, fast or slow, they've just
experienced the best.

"The Best" includes those volunteers who make this
race so great.
Who help the runners find their way, who tell them
where to wait,
And while the race is on who hand out cups of
water clear –
Those special, paper cups of liquid life – raised up,
in cheer!

So now you've learned a little more about this
famous run,
You, too, can aim to get involved in something so
much fun.
To run the race you must at least be eighteen
years of age
(In order to protect your bones while in their
growing stage),

But certainly, dear children, run the shorter races!
Find
How running strengthens everything – your legs,
lungs, mood and mind –
Infuses fresh new energy for great ideas and

Abilities and friendly games, perhaps a straight handstand.

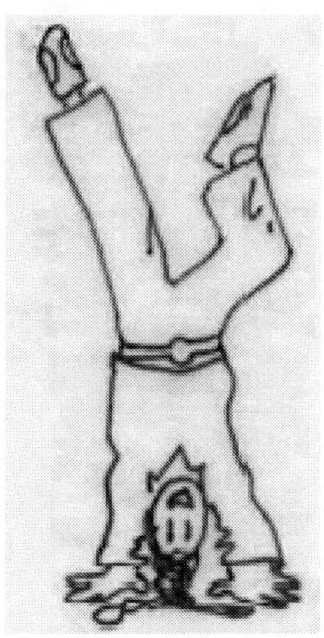

Fiona Bayly

Explore the ways to get involved with races and
events,
To fortify against those ills that exercise
prevents.
Work gently, work consistently; you'll find your
greatest wealth
Is in the state of wellness: it's the priceless gift of
health.

So meanwhile, come and lend a hand. Become a
volunteer!
Several hundred youngsters and adults throughout
the year
Have found events they'd like to do, and made good
friendships, too,
Because they know when people help each other,
dreams
come
true.

Fiona Bayly

1. Staten Island
2. Brooklyn
3. Queens
4. Manhattan
5. Bronx

A scholarly advocate for healthful recreation and a nationally ranked triathlete and road runner, the author has written and cartooned on topics ranging from nutrition to education. A graduate of Dartmouth and S.U.N.Y. Stony Brook, this Manhattan resident extols imaginative literature that invites children (and adults!) into the creative world of physical activity.

The author, a former staff member of the New York City Marathon's organizer, sees the great race as a vehicle for people of all ages to learn about the various occupations it encompasses. Inspired by the children's books Dr. Seuss, she offers this book as an original opportunity to spark children's imaginations and to tickle adults' perceptions of work and play.

The New York City Marathon, founded by Fred Lebow and today shaped by the technical brilliance of race director Alan Steinfeld, is orchestrated by the New York Road Runners, the largest running organization in the world. Its website is www.nyrrc.org.

Fiona Bayly

Fiona Bayly

Fiona Bayly

About the Author

A scholarly advocate for healthful recreation and a nationally ranked triathlete and road runner, the author has written and cartooned on topics ranging from nutrition to education. A graduate of Dartmouth and S.U.N.Y. Stony Brook, this Manhattan resident extols imaginative literature that invites children (and adults!) into the creative world of physical activity.

The author, a former staff member of the New York City Marathon's organizer, sees the great race as a vehicle for people of all ages to learn about the various occupations it encompasses. Inspired by the children's books Dr. Seuss, she offers this book as an original opportunity to spark children's imaginations and to tickle adults' perceptions of work and play.

LaVergne, TN USA
09 April 2010
178712LV00001B/194/A